BIG CITY PORT

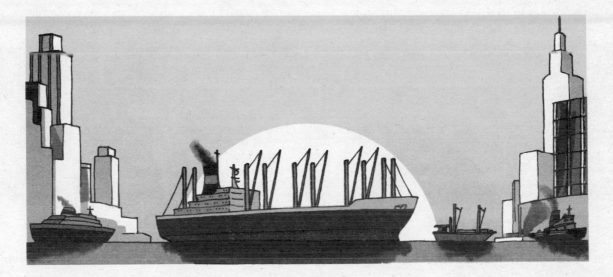

by Betsy Maestro and Ellen DelVecchio

illustrated by Giulio Maestro

SCHOLASTIC INC.
New York Toronto London Auckland Sydney

FOR ALI, DANIELA, AND MARCO

ISBN 0-590-41577-8

Text copyright © 1983 by Betsy Maestro and Ellen DelVecchio. Illustrations copyright © 1983 by Giulio Maestro. All rights reserved. This edition published by Scholastic Inc., 730 Broadway, New York, NY 10003.

12 11 10 9 8 7   4/9

Printed in the U.S.A.   08

A big city port is a busy place.
Boats and ships come into the port
to load and unload.
It is a safe place for them to dock.

Freighters, tankers, and passenger liners
are large ships that come into the port.

The smaller tugboats, ferryboats, and
fishing boats come, too.

Large ships carry heavy loads.
A freighter is bringing coffee to the city.
The tanker is coming into port loaded with oil.
The ocean liner is arriving full of passengers.

Tugboats push and pull each big ship
through the harbor to the docks.
Big ships cannot turn and move in the small places
near the piers without help.

At the dock the freighter is unloaded.
Workers use big cranes to lift the sacks
of coffee beans out of the hold and
onto the pier.

Other freighters are unloaded at nearby docks.
Many different machines are used to move
their cargoes onto the docks.
Boxes, barrels, and bales are everywhere.

Everyone is busy on the docks,
working to move the cargo.
Some of it is loaded onto trucks and trains.
The rest is moved into large
storage sheds on the pier.

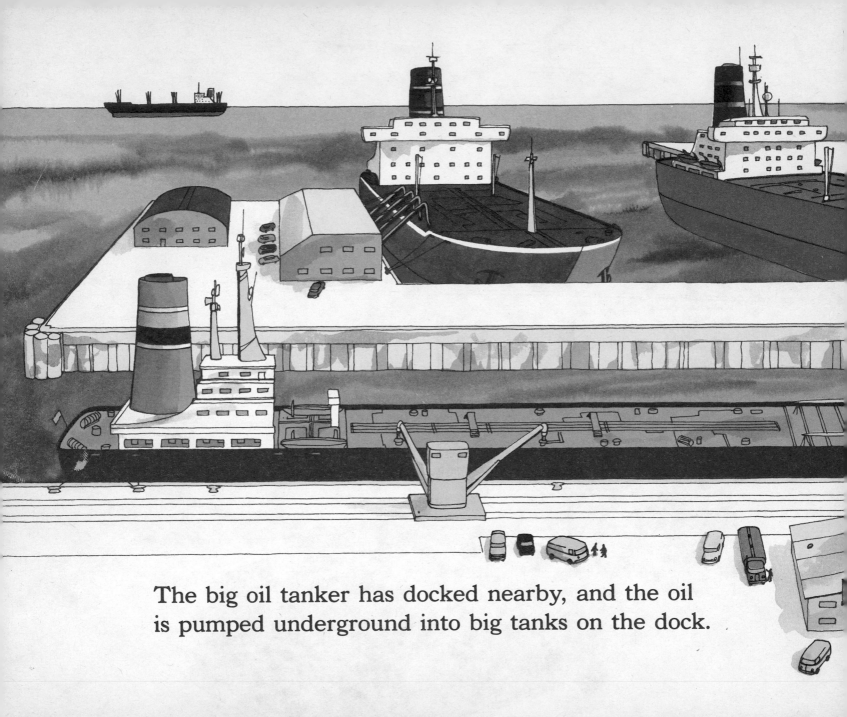

The big oil tanker has docked nearby, and the oil
is pumped underground into big tanks on the dock.

Gasoline and fruit juice are unloaded
from other tankers.

The ocean liner has docked, and the passengers are getting off.
Workers are unloading luggage.
Cars and taxis will take the people into the city.

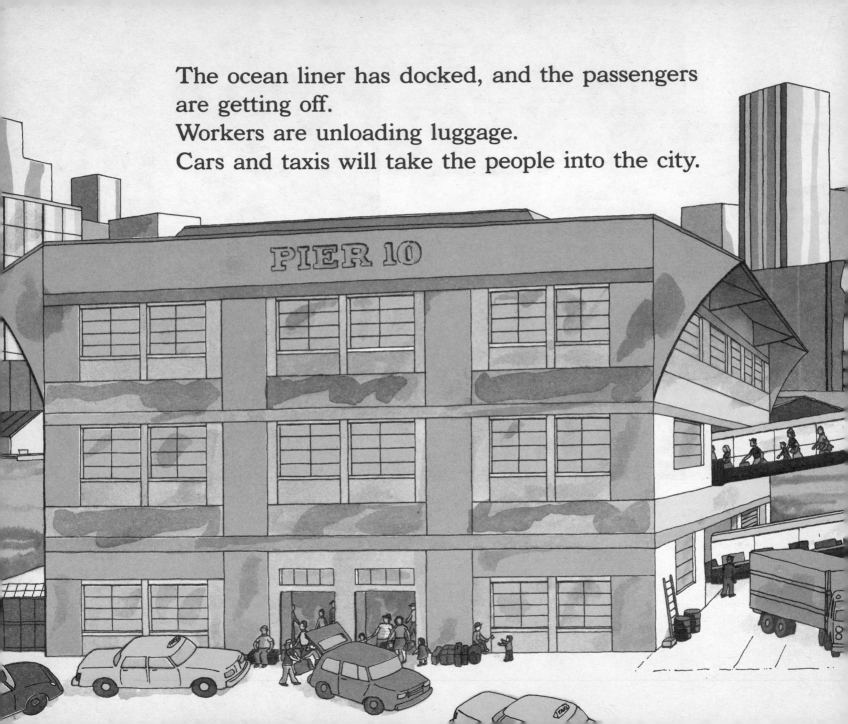

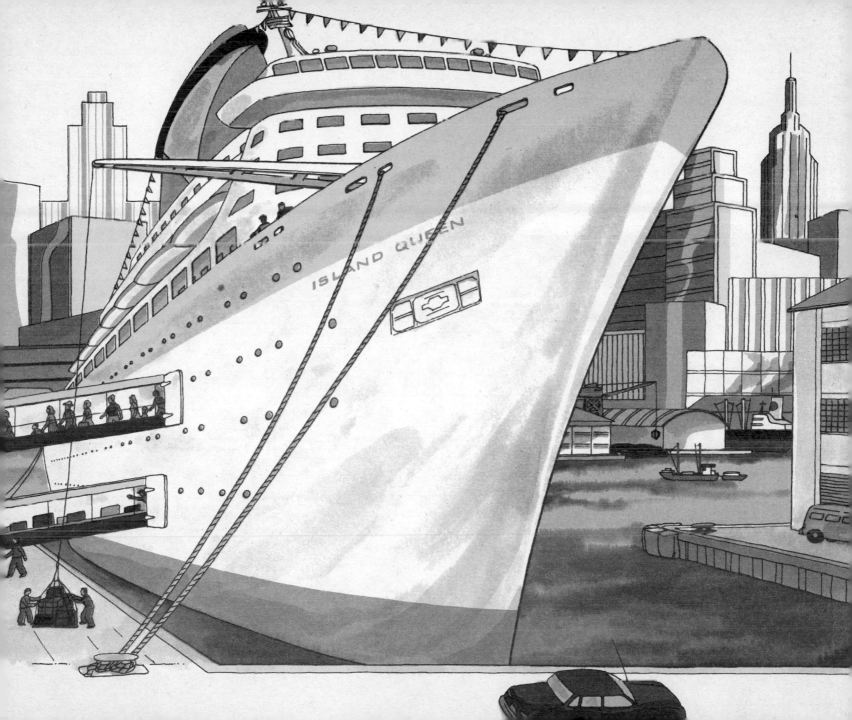

Many smaller boats come into port.
Ferryboats go back and forth across the harbor.

They carry people and cars from one side to the other.

Fishing boats go out early in the morning.
They will return full of fish at the end of the day.
The fish will be sold in markets in the city.

Many people control the traffic in a busy port.
The Captain of the Port is in charge
of all the boats and ships.

The captain on each boat or ship must follow directions and obey safety rules and signals.

There are other people who help to keep
the port safe.
Harbor police patrol the water and the piers.
Fire fighters help to put out fires and
clean up oil spills.
The fireboats are like floating fire engines.

The port never closes.
Workers are busy all day and all night.

A big city port is an important place.

At night very bright lights help them to see
so they can do their jobs.